MW01045926

NOW HIRING: FASHION

by Judy Black

Crestwood House
New York
Maxwell Macmillan Canada
Toronto
Maxwell Macmillan International
New York Oxford Singapore Sydney

Crestwood House
Macmillan Publishing Company
866 Third Avenue
New York, NY 10022

Maxwell Macmillan Canada, Inc.
1200 Eglinton Avenue East
Suite 200
Don Mills, Ontario M3C 3N1

Produced by Twelfth House Productions
Designed by R Studio T
photo credits:
cover: Model courtesy of Donna Karan, other photos by Brian Vaughan
courtesy of Donna Karan: 5, 21
Steve Vaccariello: 7, 9
Brian Vaughan: 12, 15, 18, 19, 26, 31, 33, 34, 36-37
courtesy of David & Lee: 23

Macmillan Publishing Company is part of the Maxwell Communication
Group of Companies.

First Edition

Printed in the United States of America

10 9 8 7 6 5 4 3 2 1

Library of Congress Cataloging-in-Publication Data

Black, Judy.
Fashion / by Judy Black.—1st ed.
p. cm.—(Now hiring)
Includes index.
ISBN 0-89686-791-9 ISBN 0-382-24747-7 (pbk)
Summary: An overview of the different types of jobs available in the fashion industry.
1. Fashion merchandising—Vocational guidance—Juvenile literature. 2. Models (Persons)—Vocational guidance—Juvenile literature. 3. Fashion photography—Vocational guidance—Juvenile literature. 4. Clothing trade—Vocational guidance—Juvenile literature. [1. Fashion—Vacational guidance. 2. Clothing trade—Vocational guidance. I. Title. II Series:
HD9940.A2B58 1994
687′.0688—dc20 93-4639

CONTENTS

THIS BUSINESS OF FASHION

Fashion is a multibillion dollar business. It is one of the nation's largest industries. The field offers a wide variety of opportunities. And every area is exciting.

No matter what your personality or preferences, the fashion industry has a job for you. Do you prefer to work alone? Do you like to work with a specific goal in mind? Are you at your best when working in a large group? The fashion industry has jobs for all kinds of people.

The fashion industry deals with the design, production, marketing, and distribution of clothing and accessories for men, women, and children. There is room for workers with different skills, interests, and education. Job requirements vary.

There are few gender barriers in the fashion industry. Women and men usually have an equal chance to succeed.

You don't have to attend college to get a job in fashion. Many jobs are taught in brief specialty classes. And many others can be learned through firsthand experience. Actual experience is, in fact, the best teacher. Working with experts in the field will give you invaluable hands-on practice. All you need is the desire to learn and the willingness to work hard.

In this book, you will meet some of the people who have made a career for themselves in the fashion industry. They all enjoy their work. They have insights to offer and advice for getting started. As you read, imagine what a day might be like for you if you had their job. Look at yourself and determine what your strengths are. Find out what interests you. Consider what skills you have that might help you in your chosen area. Then set some goals. This book will help you achieve them.

The fashion industry offers exciting careers in modeling, photography, sales, and more.

FASHION PHOTOGRAPHER

Nuts and Bolts of the Job

A breeze blows through the hair of three women as they pose by the railing of a cruise ship. Their clothes and makeup are perfect. Are these women tourists on their way to the Caribbean? No. They're models posing for a cruisewear fashion shoot. And it's up to fashion photographers like Steve to capture the right look in each shot.

Steve owns his own photography business. He is responsible for everything that happens on a photo shoot. "It's a group effort, but everything falls on my shoulders because I'm the one hired by the client. I'm the one looking through the camera," he says.

As soon as Steve is hired for a photo shoot, he meets with the client to find out exactly what he or she wants. "I find out what the job is going to consist of," Steve says. "Will it be black-and-white or color photography? Will it be shot in the studio or **on location**? When something is shot on location, the photos are taken outside the studio. What is the feel of the campaign?" Steve needs to know exactly what the client wants so that he can shoot the right kinds of photographs.

RELATED JOBS:
Photography assistant
Darkroom technician

Once Steve has an idea of the client's vision, he hires the **talent**. Talent is the model or models he will photograph. To find models, Steve looks through **agency books**. These books contain pictures of all the models the agency works with. Steve also uses **comp cards** when he's hiring talent. These cards feature a model's photo as well as height, weight, and clothing size.

A fashion photographer shooting on location.

While Steve is choosing the models he's going to work with, he's also busy readying the set. "I usually have the entire set built according to what the client wants, whether it's part of a room or a **white seamless**." A white seamless background is exactly that—white and completely smooth. To achieve this look, Steve builds a "wall" with a giant roll of white paper. The paper runs from the ceiling to the floor.

When it's time for the shoot, Steve hires a **hair stylist** and a **makeup stylist**. The stylists make the models look their best. While the models are groomed, Steve puts the finishing touches on the set. He makes sure the lighting is right, takes trial shots, or finds a last-minute prop.

When Steve works outside his studio, he usually sends a **photography assistant** to scout out locations. The location must meet the specific needs of the photograph. Of course, weather plays a role in outside shots. "We always have a backup studio or a backup date if we're shooting on location," Steve explains.

Steve usually works with a crew. The size of the crew depends on his **budget**. A budget is the amount of money that's been set aside for a shoot. The bigger the budget, the more people Steve can hire. "We did a shoot for one client that had a big budget. We cast people from all over the country," he says. "When you have a lot of money to spend, you can get a top-notch crew."

Most models are paid by the hour. So Steve doesn't take a lunch break during a shoot. "There's no time for it," Steve explains. "These models are paid on a time basis. The client is always trying to watch the budget, so I have to get things done as quickly as I can."

After the photograph is shot, it is processed. Then the photos are put on a **proof sheet**. This is a sheet with a number of small photos. The client uses a proof sheet to choose the photos he or she wants to use.

Steve loves being a fashion photographer. He likes visualizing a project and watching it develop into a fashion advertisement. And he enjoys dealing with the unexpected things that may come up. "The end result is always worth it," he says.

Have You Got What It Takes?

Being a fashion photographer includes more than taking photographs. You must be able to visualize an idea and see it through to the finish—all with a style of your own.

"ULTIMATELY, PHOTOGRAPHY COMES FROM YOUR HEART AND SOUL."

A photographer takes a light reading before shooting photographs.

Steve's first photography job was working as a medical photographer at a hospital. He took pictures of wounded patients. To forget the sight of all that blood, he started taking fashion photos. "I couldn't stand all the pain and suffering," Steve says. "I used fashion and beauty as my outlet."

Initially, Steve took fashion pictures on his own time. But after a while he decided to leave the hospital and start his own business.

Unbelievably, Steve has never taken a photography class. He just picked up the camera and learned from trial and error. "Ultimately, photography comes from your heart and soul," says Steve. "That's what you can't get from school. School can teach you the technical side. But clients are looking for photos that have feeling, that have emotion. The shots have to be unpredictable and different."

To learn about fashion photography, Steve watched other photographers at work. He also looked at models, lighting, and fashion ads. "I put all of these things into my creative mind and decided what I wanted to produce as an artist," Steve tells us.

If you want to be a fashion photographer, you should be goal-oriented. You must also be organized. There are many details to take care of when you're planning a photo shoot.

Patience is another requirement. Everything has to be just right before a picture can be taken. And it's important to have good people skills, too. A photographer has to make sure that the people he or she works with are comfortable. That way the model, crew, and others can do their best work.

To build your skills as a photographer, you should get your hands on a 35-millimeter camera. You shouldn't use an automatic, autofocus camera. You need to learn how to set the adjustments by hand. "Taking pictures should be something you think about, not something you set automatically," Steve says.

And it helps to have someone to practice on. Shoot pictures of your friends or family. This will give you experience with different lighting, settings, and people. And you'll learn how to focus on key elements of a photograph.

Once you've taken photos that you're pleased with, start building your **portfolio**. A portfolio is a collection of your best work. Photographers show portfolios to potential clients.

"TAKING PICTURES SHOULD BE SOMETHING YOU THINK ABOUT."

It's also a good idea to look at ads in magazines. Study the pictures. Decide which photos appeal to you and which don't. Or take a photography class. This will teach you the technical side of photography. It will also give you a chance to compare your photos with other students'.

And finally, get involved with a photography organization, like the American Society for Magazine Photographers. These organizations have meetings and workshops that will help you expand your knowledge. They'll give you the chance to be around other photographers. And soon you may be shooting photographs professionally yourself.

FASHION DESIGNER

Nuts and Bolts of the Job

You're in a dressing room trying on a brightly colored sweater. You pull it over your head, look in the mirror, and smile. It fits you perfectly—right down to the way the sleeves hang.

Coincidence? Hardly. Fashion designers like Isabelle make sure that the clothing they create meets certain standards. Isabelle, who knits sweaters on a loom, pays attention to every detail.

Isabelle begins a project by drawing **rough sketches**. These drawings show the basic idea of the item she plans to make. When Isabelle is happy with the sketches, she develops a **paper pattern**. A paper pattern is like a model of the garment, separated into pieces (such as a sleeve).

RELATED JOBS:
Assistant designer
Costume designer
Pattern grader

Using the paper pattern, Isabelle creates a **sample**. A sample gives a designer a good idea of how the final garment will look. Most designers

A designer at work on a loom

make samples out of **muslin**, an inexpensive material. Isabelle drapes the strong, sheer muslin over a mannequin to see how the sweater will fit.

Next, Isabelle makes a sweater out of the real yarn. She checks it carefully to make sure it's just right. Sometimes she makes alterations—small changes to the garment.

Most of Isabelle's designs are made from rayon yarns, which are very light. She uses a knitting loom, and everything is handmade. Even the edging and the buttons are done by hand. Isabelle usually crochets these extra pieces. Crocheting is needlework done with a one-hooked needle.

When Isabelle is designing and knitting clothes, she pays attention to body size. This is important, because no two figures are the same. Designers must consider how a change in size will affect the garment they are creating. Will a design look good on a tall person *and* on a short person? Will this sweater look as nice on a big person as it does on a small person? To help answer questions like these, Isabelle uses her friends as models. She invites them to try on clothes she's working on.

Designers also think about who will buy their clothing. "Knowing who your clients are is part of developing your self-expression and style," she explains. "You're never going to appeal to everybody. I think it's fun to appeal to a small group and be really creative with your clothing."

The fashion industry, like the year, has four seasons: spring, summer, winter, and fall. Therefore, designers are expected to create four different **fashion lines**, or collections, each year. While you are in the store shopping for spring clothes, Isabelle is hard at work on her fall line. "I'm designing and getting my fall collection ready in January," she says.

Since Isabelle doesn't have an assistant, her days are long and hectic. Some last 20 hours. But it's time well spent. Her clothing starts at $250 and goes up. Her time pays off.

Have You Got What It Takes?

Creating clothes that look good requires talent, vision, and style. These are three things a fashion designer must possess.

Isabelle wanted to be a fashion designer since she was a child. When she was eight years old, her mother enrolled her in a sewing

"I'M DESIGNING AND GETTING MY FALL COLLECTION READY IN JANUARY."

class. That's where she learned how to read a pattern and put pieces of fabric together.

By the time Isabelle was in high school, she was redesigning clothes she bought at stores. She would take an ordinary blouse, cut it apart, and sew the pieces together in a new way. Isabelle was designing and didn't even realize it! "I was changing the clothes I bought for years before I realized that I was designing clothes," she says.

Isabelle never studied design in school. She considers herself self-taught. "At first I wasn't confident enough. But I'm very creative."

Isabelle recommends working in a boutique if you're interested in fashion design. That's where she learned that people wear clothes differently. "I learned a lot about how women wear clothes. I found out that not everybody looks the same in a piece of clothing. For example, some women don't look good in scoop necks."

If you want to be a fashion designer, you need determination. "I think it's very important to have drive," says Isabelle. "Especially if you're self-taught. It's valuable to have an education, but in some ways I'm glad I don't. Teaching myself has allowed me to discover things on my own."

A fashion designer must develop a strong sense of self-expression right from the start. So learn to sew and make your own clothes. Go to the fabric store and become familiar with different fabrics and colors. Look through pattern books. Then buy patterns and make some changes. And when you buy clothes, add a few touches to personalize them.

It's also a good idea to browse through fashion magazines. It's not important to know the names of the designs or designers. What you are looking for is what you do and don't like about a specific

"IT'S ALL ABOUT DEVELOPING YOUR STYLE."

A fashion designer and one of her assistants piece together a sweater.

garment. “Part of fashion design is to be inspired by what you’re looking at,” Isabelle explains. “It’s not that I’ll copy what I see. If I like the way the colors flow, I’ll incorporate them into something else. It’s all about developing your style.”

Surround yourself with fashion photos or illustrations that inspire you. Then set up a time and place to practice your designs. “You have to set aside time, says Isabelle. “Know that between these hours and during these days, even if you don’t feel like it, you’re going to sit down and design, sew, knit, or whatever.” If you keep at it, someday you may be a fashion designer like Isabelle!

PRODUCTION ASSISTANT

Nuts and Bolts of the Job

You're browsing through your favorite store when a belt catches your eye. The brass shines. And the leather is so soft. It will look great with your new pants.

Long before that belt reached the store, it was a product idea. It had to be put together, piece by piece. Then it had to be shipped to the right place. Production assistants like Luke make sure that the production and shipping go smoothly.

Luke works at the Donna Karan design company. He deals with accessories—handbags, belts, jewelry, scarves, and hats. Each item starts out as a designer's idea. That idea is sketched out, and then a sample is manufactured. The samples are made of **salpe**, which is an inexpensive rubberized fabric. Using salpe saves on production costs. It allows the designer to make changes without spending a lot of money.

When the designer is happy with the sample, it's ready to be manufactured. Luke makes sure that the manufacturers have the materials they need to go ahead with production.

Some manufacturers are easy to work with. For example, the Korean company that makes most of Donna Karan's handbags orders its own materials. "I tell them how many handbags I need and they send me the finished product," Luke says. "It's great."

Other manufacturers need more help. "Sometimes I have to order every little nut and bolt," Luke says. He orders materials from different companies. Most of these companies provide the Donna Karan Company with materials on a regular basis. For example, Luke orders certain leathers from a shop in Italy.

Aside from providing the manufacturer with materials for production, Luke helps create the **line list**. The line list is like a catalog. It lists information about each item in a season's line, including price, fabric, colors, and style number. Stores that sell Donna Karan accessories use the line list to place orders. They tell Luke how many of each item they want, and Luke orders the products from the manufacturer.

Once an accessory is put together, Luke has to make sure it reaches its final destination—the warehouse. The warehouse stores and ships all the company's accessories. Luke's company has two warehouses—one in New Jersey and one in the Netherlands.

RELATED JOBS:
Merchandising assistant
Pattern grader
Spreader

Luke spends a good deal of his day at a computer, entering in orders that stores have placed. Since he works with shops and manufacturers all over the world, he has to look at each order carefully. "If an item is manufactured in Italy and sold in France, it would be silly to ship it to the warehouse in the United States and then reship it to Europe," he explains.

Luke spends about ten hours a day at the office. But when the company is working on a new season's line, he works evenings and weekends, too. He has to make sure that the new accessories are ready for each season's fashion show, where they will be introduced. "I work really long hours trying to get everything together," Luke tells us.

In spite of the hectic times, Luke enjoys being a production assistant. "It's neat to watch an accessory go from a designer's idea to a product we sell," he says.

"SOMETIMES I HAVE TO ORDER EVERY LITTLE NUT AND BOLT."

A production assistant examines fabric samples.

Have You Got What It Takes?

Being a production assistant is rewarding. You keep track of a product from start to finish. And it's an excellent position to get an overview of the manufacturing process.

Luke's first step into the fashion industry was a job as a retail salesperson. "It's a matter of getting out there and working anywhere in retail," he says. "You get to know certain things about the industry."

As Luke became more interested in fashion, he discovered that there were many different areas he could explore. Eventually he opted for the production side of the business. “I’m a structured person,” he says. “I feel better when things are really organized.”

A production assistant must be able to keep track of many details. He or she is the link between the design room and the factory. Good math and organizational skills are a must. “I started out with a small company, basically running the office,” says Luke. “This taught me how to organize.” Typing, data entry, and computer skills are also helpful.

Production assistants work with all kinds of people. And that’s not always easy. “I work with many different people from many different places,” Luke says. “I have to realize that when someone is moody, it’s not directed at me. I can’t take things personally.”

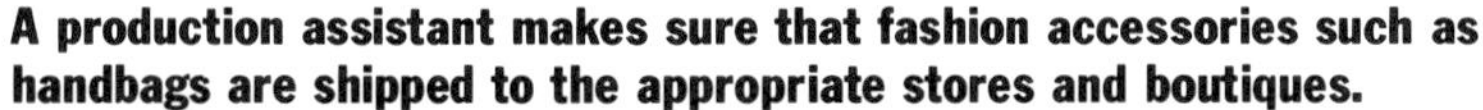

A production assistant makes sure that fashion accessories such as handbags are shipped to the appropriate stores and boutiques.

If you want to be a production assistant, "take accessories you like apart. Then put them back together the way you would like to see them," Luke suggests. If you sew or make your own clothing, you might be doing this without even realizing it. If you don't know how to sew, take a course in school or at a Y or community center.

It's also a good idea to take computer or typing classes. A production assistant spends a good deal of time entering orders into a computer. And get a job in a retail store. It will give you a chance to work with different clothing, accessories, and people. The courses and the work experience will teach you about the manufacturing process.

MODEL

Nuts and Bolts of the Job

You're paging through a catalog when you see a beautiful outfit. It's sleek and sophisticated—just what you've been looking for. And you know it will make you feel as attractive as the person wearing it in the catalog.

Connie, a professional model, is responsible for making sure that you see more than clothing in a photograph. "A model displays a fashion item physically, and with an attitude," Connie says. "Whether on the runway or in a picture, you have to bring across that what you're wearing is a wonderful garment."

A model can be asked to wear anything from formal clothing to a hand-painted sweatshirt. Even if the garment is not something Connie would choose to wear, she has to look comfortable in it. "You really have to be a bit of an actress," Connie tells us.

A model shows off a fall coat against a white seamless background.

There are many different kinds of modeling. Some models work in front of a camera. Some do **formal modeling**. Formal modeling is done on a runway, in fashion shows and showrooms. Others do **informal modeling**. Informal modeling can be done almost anywhere—at a store or in a person's home. Some models even work in a specific store, modeling a line of clothing. But most working models make their living posing for catalogs. "Most models work for local retailers," Connie explains. This means they work for stores in their hometown. They are photographed wearing different clothes the store sells.

RELATED JOBS:
Fashion stylist
Hair stylist
Makeup stylist

Only a few models—about 2 percent—make their living doing big-contract accounts. Cindy Crawford, Christie Brinkley, and Linda Evangelista are considered supermodels. But for every famous model, there are thousands of people who make their living doing small-scale modeling.

Models usually start their careers when they are 17 or 18 years old. But most of the models you see in catalogs are a bit older, generally in their mid-20s.

How do models get their jobs? With the help of agencies. Modeling agencies feature all their models in agency books, which are sent to clients. Clients use agency books to choose the model or models they want to work with. "We also have comp cards," Connie says. "These list our measurements and clothing sizes." It's important for clients to have information about the models. They need to know what size dress and shoes to have ready.

Connie checks in with her modeling agency in Chicago every Monday. They let her know where she is expected to be, on what day. "I'd say an average workweek for a model is three days," says

"YOU REALLY HAVE TO BE A BIT OF AN ACTRESS."

Connie. "If it's very busy, you might be working all five."

On a typical catalog shoot, Connie is photographed in several outfits—sometimes as many as 100. She might be photographed in the department store. She might be photographed in a local studio. Or she might be photographed on location.

For Connie, the best part of being a model is location work. When she's working on location, she usually gets to travel. She's done location work in Alaska, Key West, Florida, and just about everywhere in between. One of her best jobs was a photo shoot in San Diego. "It was a five-day, all-expenses-paid job," she says. "And I was paid my regular daily salary. But I ended up working only one of those days. So I got to play the rest of the time." Not bad!

Soft focus and a reclining pose help Connie display a colorful dress.

The only thing Connie doesn't like about modeling is that it sometimes creates a false sense of what the body should look like. "Some models think they have to be so skinny," she says. "You should find the weight you look good at and maintain it."

Have You Got What It Takes?

Being a model is exciting. You travel. You wear the latest fashions. You have your hair and makeup done. And clothes are tailored to fit you.

Connie started modeling when she finished high school. She was working as a secretary. Her boss's husband ran a small modeling agency. The boss suggested that Connie send photos to him.

Connie worked with that agency for about six months. During that time she built her portfolio. A model's portfolio contains a collection of his or her work.

After a while Connie went to a bigger agency. Working with a larger agency made Connie more visible. That's when the phone started ringing. "Once you get your picture where people can see it, clients start asking, 'Who is this person?' And they'll call and ask for you."

Connie lives in Chicago. But she has had steady work in many cities across the United States. She has worked in New York, Dallas, Chicago, Cleveland, and Atlanta. She has even worked in Paris. "A model can live anywhere," Connie says. "You can fly where the work is—especially if your agency is in a major market," Connie says.

A model must have an outgoing personality. After all, you're a salesperson, selling yourself. You have to convince people you are the best person for the job.

"A MODEL DISPLAYS A FASHION ITEM PHYSICALLY, AND WITH AN ATTITUDE."

"And you have to be professional," Connie says. "You have to work with a lot of different people—adapt to every situation." A model always has to arrive at a shoot ready to work.

There's no denying that a pleasing face and a well-groomed look are part of the job. If modeling is something that interests you, you must take care of yourself. You may want to work out and watch your diet. Do cardiovascular and weight work to build muscle tone. And stay away from sweets and fatty foods (that's good advice even if you're not a model).

Although appearance is important in modeling, you do not have to be tall and thin to be a model. People of all sizes and shapes buy clothing. So catalogs and store fliers need models for large sizes, too.

"Have someone take pictures of you in different clothes," Connie advises. "Study the pictures and decide what makes you look good. And figure out how to hide your weak areas. That way, when you walk into an agency, they'll know you are serious." Good advice from someone who knows!

RETAIL MARKETING ASSISTANT

Nuts and Bolts of the Job

You're at a fashion show in an upscale showroom. A new line of evening wear is being introduced. Models stroll up and down the runway in sleek, glimmering dresses. Music hums over the speakers. And the lights glow. Who makes fashion events like this one successful?

A retail marketing assistant makes sure that clothing samples are shipped to the location of a fashion event.

It's the job of marketing assistants like Lynne. She promotes her company's clothing in different stores. "A retail marketing assistant works as a coordinator," Lynne says. She coordinates clothing, people, and places.

On any given day Lynne might speak with the editors of a magazine that is working on an event with her company. She might book, or hire, models. Lynne also comes up with themes for fashion shows. Almost every fashion show has a theme. The theme goes with the clothes that are being shown. It ties the decorations, the food, and other features together.

Before an event Lynne makes sure that clothing samples are transferred from the warehouse to the location of that event. The event might be in Los Angeles or Philadelphia. Lynne's company works with stores all over the country.

Lynne also makes sure that invitations have been sent to local and national newspapers and magazines. She hires musicians or arranges for taped music. And she makes sure that caterers have been hired.

RELATED JOBS:
Fashion show coordinator
Promotions assistant

Another part of Lynne's job is to oversee the ordering, shipping, and displaying of promotional items. Sometimes her company gives out token gifts at an event. The item might be a key chain or a ballpoint pen. Lynne orders these items from a manufacturer and makes sure that they are ready before the event.

Each store that Lynne works with has a budget—a certain amount of money set aside for fashion events. She has to make sure that each event stays within the store's budget.

As you can tell, Lynne's job involes a number of different tasks. But she enjoys being a retail marketing assistant. "My days are never the same," she says. "I like the variety and creativity. There's freedom for you to pick and choose how you want to set up an event."

Have You Got What It Takes?

Retail marketing assistants coordinate people, places, and clothes. They have to take care of many details and stay within an event's budget. If you're an organized person, retail marketing assistant could be the job for you.

Lynne started her fashion career as a salesclerk at a clothing store. "In high school I worked at the Gap," she says. "I started when I was 14 and worked until I moved to New York. I was ready to quit a few times, but I knew I wanted to do something in the fashion industry, so I held on to the job."

Lynne moved to New York to get closer to the fashion industry. When she took a paid **internship** at the Anne Klein fashion company, she got her foot in the door. "A friend recommended me," she tells us. "I jumped from the sales end of the business into the marketing end, and I love it."

Doing an internship and developing contacts is something that Lynne strongly recommends. "Take advantage of an internship or the people you know," Lynne says. "That's the best way to build up your résumé. And it's the way to get yourself in the door somewhere."

Although Lynne works with budgets, she feels there is no special need to take math classes beyond the high school level. In fact, doing well in math isn't all that important. "I really didn't do well in my math classes," Lynne confesses. "They were my weak points in school."

There's no denying that creativity plays an important role in being a retail marketing assistant. So it's a good idea to take classes in sewing, art, or shop. You might even want to take pattern making. "If you want to get into this field, you're going to have to find out about it," Lynne advises. "If your high school offers these types of classes, take them."

You might also want to assist in producing school or community plays. Volunteering for a theater will give you a chance to work with clothing in a "set-up" atmosphere.

"A RETAIL MARKETING ASSISTANT WORKS AS A COORDINATOR."

Another good idea would be to get a job at a retail store. A retail marketing assistant has to work with clothing and people. And working at your favorite clothing store may give you the chance to do both. The experience may help you become a retail marketing assistant like Lynne.

IMAGE CONSULTANT

Nuts and Bolts of the Job

Do you have a natural sense of style? Do you shop for friends and family? Do coworkers, friends, or relatives ask, "Where did you get that dress?" "How come you always look so wonderful?" or "Will you come shopping with me?"

If you enjoy shopping and have a flair for fashion, image consulting may be for you.

Virginia is an image consultant. An **image consultant** works to bring out the best look in a person, or maybe even an entire company. Virginia deals with color, fashion sense, and fabric. She also works with voice and body language. "An image consultant uses fashion to improve a person's self-esteem," Virginia says.

There is an ideal chain of events for image consulting. First individuals find out what colors are most flattering to them. They can look for these colors while shopping.

The second part of a consultation is cosmetic. Of course, if you are consulting a man, this part of the job is not necessary. But for a woman, cosmetic consulting can be very helpful. It teaches her about skin care and the correct application of different types of makeup. She also learns what colors are best for her face.

Next comes a **closet audit.** An image consultant goes into the client's closet to see what he or she owns. "We want to see what people have—what we can add to," Virginia explains.

Another kind of consultation is **figure typing.** It involves looking at a person and determining his or her body type. A person with a well-defined waist area has an X-shape. Someone with straight sides is an H-shape. A pear-shaped person is narrower above the waist than below. "Image consultants determine what kind of body a person has and then figure out which **silhouettes** work best with that shape," Virginia explains. Silhouettes are the outlines of clothes.

RELATED JOBS:
Personal shopper
Makeup stylist

Consultants also work with **style analysis.** The consultant studies the client's coloring, figure, features, and personality to come up with an appropriate clothing type. Some people may look best in classic clothing. A classic style features straight lines. Other people prefer a more glamorous look. A glamorous style consists of broad angles. And a romantic style features clothes that emphasize curves. "I look at everything about a person's physical appearance and help him or her come up with a style that's just right," Virginia says.

In addition to doing personal analyses, many image consultants work with companies. Virginia presents seminars and corporate training programs. And she gives lectures about fashion. She explains how looking good helps people become more successful. "If you look good, you feel good about yourself and your job," she says.

As an image consultant, you must decide who your clients will be. Will you cater to professionals or athletes? men or women? This is an important decision for an image consultant.

Once you decide who your clients will be, you have to find them. "You don't have to do a lot of image consulting to make some money," Virginia says. "The hard part is getting the clients—getting and keeping them."

Virginia's day usually involves some reading. She reads *Women's Wear Daily*, a newspaper that keeps her up-to-date on fashion trends. Keeping up with the trends is an important part of an image consultant's job. She also reads magazines she thinks her clients would read. Virginia works long hours because she has to accommodate her clients' schedules. She may have to meet some clients over breakfast or go to a client's home in the evening.

Although Virginia's days are long, she has the freedom to create her own schedules. And she decides how much to charge. Virginia is her own boss!

An image consultant explains the season's colors to a group of clients.

Have You Got What It Takes?

Virginia became interested in fashion when she was working in a bank. "I came in contact with many executives," says Virginia. "The ones who dressed the part were very successful. Some of them needed help with their looks, which led me into image consulting."

To find out more about image consulting, Virginia took an adult education course in color analysis. The woman who taught the class was looking for an assistant. So Virginia trained with her in the evenings. It wasn't long before Virginia left her banking position to become a full-time image consultant.

An image consultant has to develop his or her own sense of style. You don't need a degree from a fashion school to be an image consultant. But you do need to be fashionable. So pay attention to how you look. Try to be well groomed at all times.

If you want to be an image consultant, you'll need to decide who your clients will be. Then you should learn as much about the styles and habits of those people as you can. Most of the people who hire image consultants are business professionals. To learn about professional men and women, you should read magazines like *Forbes* or *BusinessWeek*.

No matter what area you specialize in, you have to be aware of everything related to image. "Image consulting is one of the few fields in the fashion industry that use business, communication, and visual skills all at once," Virginia says.

Look for schools in your area that offer image consulting programs. High schools sponsoring adult education classes usually have a few. Community colleges also offer courses. A class in line, design, or fabric will be helpful. Or take a business class.

"THE HARD PART IS GETTING THE CLIENTS-GETTING AND KEEPING THEM

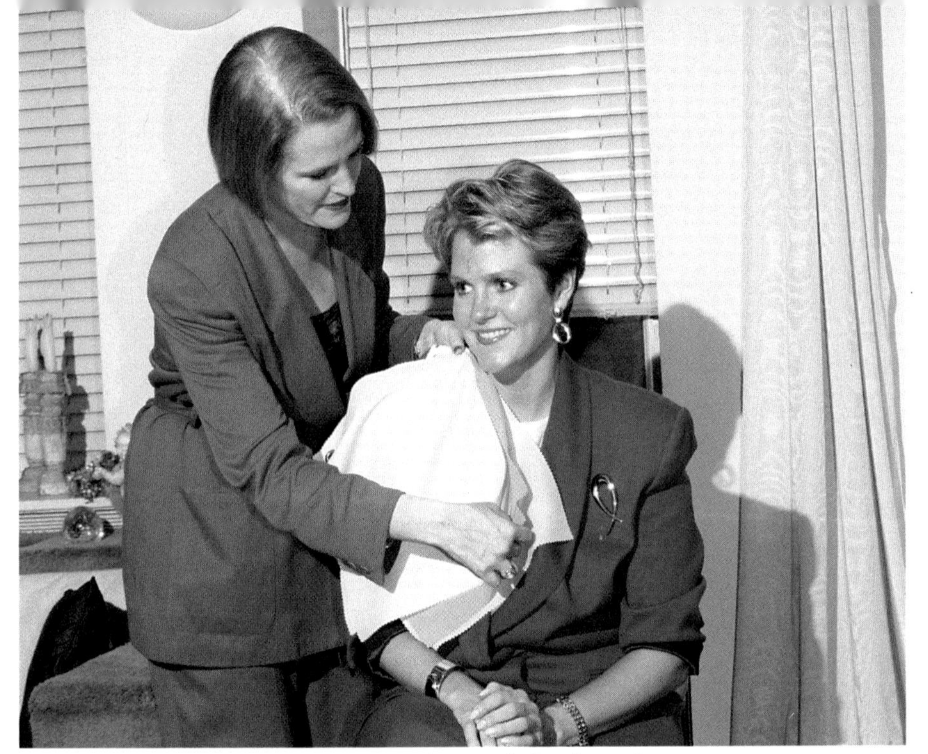

An image consultant helping a client learn what colors she wears best

Also, read plenty of fashion magazines. Take what you learn from these magazines and work on your friends' wardrobes. Or you can volunteer to work at fashion shows given at local stores. The experiences will give you a chance to see how different styles of clothes look on different people.

SHOWROOM SALESPERSON

Nuts and Bolts of the Job

Don't worry about a thing! He knows your size. He knows your coloring. He knows about your busy life-style. And he can help you find the latest fashions that are perfect for a job interview—or a trip to Peru.

Ian works in the showroom of an internationally known retail

A showroom salesperson stays in touch with his clients via the telephone.

store. It's his job to make sure that the customer gets the best service possible.

The women who shop at Ian's store have a strong sense of style—they know about clothes. Ian must be able to answer their questions. He must know exactly what each garment is made of. He has to keep up with new styles and buzzwords. And, of course, he must know how to sell his products.

Each customer has specific needs. Part of Ian's job is to know what those needs are. Does the customer travel? Is she a working woman? Or is she a homemaker? "I have to have what's right for my customers," Ian says. That usually means offering the latest styles and the highest quality clothing.

RELATED JOBS:
Visual merchandiser
Buyer
Comparison shopper

The first thing Ian does each day is to check his **client book.** The book tells him which clients are coming in, and when. "First and foremost, I have to take care of who I have coming in," he says. Ian does a lot of planning for customers who have made appointments to shop in the store. And since every customer is different, he prepares for each one in a particular way. He might have a whole line of clothing ready to show a customer. He might choose just a few items if a customer is very busy. Or he might make reservations to take a customer to lunch.

If Ian doesn't have anyone coming in, he makes phone calls. He might call clients to discuss new clothes his store will be offering. He might telephone the warehouse to order merchandise. Or he might make follow-up calls to see how his customers are enjoying their purchases.

Ian also takes care of walk-in customers. "If someone walks into the store, we do everything we can to familiarize them with the line, the clothing, and the type of service that we offer," he explains.

A showroom salesperson specializes in knowing a client's personal fashion tastes.

To keep his clients up-to-date on the store's newest items, Ian sends out catalogs and pamphlets. He also writes thank-you notes to his clients.

After all his customers are taken care of, Ian works on managing the store itself. His store shows spring/summer clothes, and fall/winter clothes. New merchandise is constantly arriving. Ian makes sure that everything is displayed in an inviting manner.

Although Ian doesn't work on a **commission,** he has monthly sales goals. And each sale, whether in the store or on the phone, brings Ian a little closer to that goal.

Not every customer who walks through the door makes a purchase. Sometimes people just can't find anything they like. And if Ian has had a long day, a missed sale can depress him. "You think, 'Gosh, what have I done?' You have to remember it's not a reflection of you or the store. But it can be discouraging," he admits.

In spite of the discouraging moments, Ian enjoys being a showroom salesperson. He likes taking care of his customers and knowing that they're satisfied. "If I make customers feel attractive, I feel satisfied. That's the best part of sales," he says.

Have You Got What It Takes?

As soon as Ian got his first part-time job in fashion retail sales, he knew he wanted to make a career of selling clothes. After high school he got a job in the shipping and receiving department of a national retail store. He unpacked boxes and hung the merchandise in the store.

"I HAVE TO HAVE WHAT'S RIGHT FOR MY CUSTOMERS."

Ian worked his way through various departments and positions. His ability to talk to many different kinds of customers helped him move up in the fashion industry. "You cannot be afraid to talk to people if you want to do sales. You have to know how to communicate with all sorts of people," he says.

A salesperson must be confident and knowledgeable. If a customer has a question, you should be able to answer it. If you're nervous or timid, customers will be less likely to buy your merchandise.

It also helps to have a sense of humor. When things get hectic or a day goes by without a sale, you have to be positive. "Laughter is always the best medicine, no matter what happens," Ian tells us.

The best way to get into sales is to get a job at a retail store. "It doesn't matter if you're a stockperson," Ian says. "You can make yourself more than that by getting involved and developing a sense of how the store is run." So apply for a job at a nearby clothing store. Once you've been hired, offer to help out in as many areas as you can.

Look through fashion magazines to find out what the latest styles are. Then head to the mall with your friends. Browse through the stores and talk about the clothes you see.

While you're shopping, notice the salespeople who help you. Do they seem knowledgeable? Are they helpful? Are they too pushy? Being an experienced shopper will make you a better salesperson. Just be careful not to spend all your money while you're doing research!

"IF I MAKE CUSTOMERS FEEL ATTRACTIVE, I FEEL SATISFIED."

FOUR THINGS TO REMEMBER NO MATTER WHAT FASHION JOB YOU WANT

1. Do your homework.

Fashion industry groups, such as the Men's Fashion Association of America, can supply you with information about men's fashion. And educational courses and programs are offered by schools like the Fashion Institute of Technology.

The library is a good place to find information about jobs in the fashion industry. Reference books are full of information about different areas in fashion. It's also a good idea to talk to your high school guidance counselor. He or she will be able to help you find out about internships, jobs, and programs in the fashion industry.

2. Get yourself out there.

Entry-level positions are a great way to get started in the fashion industry. Find out what positions are available and what the qualifications are. If the company you are interested in working for doesn't have a paid opening, find out if it offers internships. Most internships won't pay much. But the experience you'll be getting is priceless.

Before you apply for a position, make sure you have a résumé. A résumé should include your name, address, and phone number. It should state your career goals, your level of education, the schools you've attended, and any related work experience you may have. It's also a good idea to include any special activities you have participated in, like editing your school newspaper or serving as wardrobe coordinator for school plays. Skills such as sewing, typing, computers, foreign languages, or mastery of your parents' 35 millimeter camera should also be noted.

Be sure to include a cover letter when you send your résumé. A cover letter is a brief note that states why you are interested in seeking a particular job. A sample résumé is included at the end of this chapter.

When you go for an interview, dress up a bit. Add a colorful tie or a bright pin to your suit or dress—this is the fashion industry!

Answer all the questions the interviewer asks you. And feel free to ask any questions you may have. Sure, your interviewer is looking for the best person for the position. But you are looking for the best position for you.

Once you have your first job or internship, learn as much as possible. Keep your eyes and ears open. Ask questions. Watch the people you work with. See how they do their jobs. And offer to help out in different areas. You'll see other sides of the fashion industry.

3. Find a mentor.

No matter what area of the fashion industry you are interested in, you should try to learn from someone who knows the business. So find a mentor—someone who will advise you and teach you what he or she knows. Watch your mentor work, and ask questions. Discuss where you want to go in the industry. The information your mentor gives you will be helpful to you in reaching your goal.

Perhaps your mentor can help you find a job, too. Fashion is an industry that hires people not only because of their skills but also because of who they have worked with. The more people you know, the better chance you'll have to land the job of your dreams.

4. Work your way up.

There are millions of people working in the fashion industry, and many more who want to become involved. When you begin your career, you should be prepared to work for little or no money. As your skills increase, so will your pay.

Starting a career can be tough. You'll have good days and bad days. But don't get discouraged. Everyone has to start somewhere. Keep working toward your goal. You'll get there.

Fashion is a growing and changing industry. There are numerous job opportunities. For every job described in this book, there are hundreds more out there. And new jobs in the fashion industry are being created every day. No two careers are the same. There are no rules to go by. Pick an area that interests you and see how you like it. In the fashion industry, anything goes. So get out there and get busy!

Anne Allen O'Brien
1326 First Street
New Orleans, LA 70118
(504) 555-1234

Objective	To obtain an entry-level position in fashion production
Education	Louise S. McGehee High School, New Orleans, class of 1994
Work Experience	Retail salesclerk, The Gap, New Orleans Part-time, September 1992 to June 1993. Operated cash register, built displays, helped with bookkeeping. Retail salesclerk, Pasta, New Orleans Full-time, June 1992 to September 1992. Advised customers, stocked merchandise, built display structures, filled in for cashier. Other part-time jobs: Babysitting, tailoring, housecleaning for local residents
Skills	Knowledge of computers Experience in home economics Ability to adapt to any situation
Activities	Junior varsity football cheerleader, 2 years Varsity field hockey team, 2 years (captain, 1 year) Glee Club, 2 years
Personal Interests	Fashion, sewing, music, skateboarding

GLOSSARY

agency book A book that pictures the models a specific agency works with. Agency books are sent out to clients.

assistant designer A person who helps the designer create his or her fashion ideas.

budget The amount of money set aside for a project.

buyer A person who purchases merchandise to be sold in retail stores and decides how much it will cost.

client book A book containing a list of a salesperson's clients. Information includes customers' past buys, current wardrobe, life-style, and taste in clothes.

closet audit An image consultant's examination of a client's clothes.

commission A fee paid to an employee for selling a particular item.

comp card A card with a model's photograph and statistics, such as height, weight, and clothing size.

comparison shopper A person who researches the competition's merchandise, sales, and promotion of products.

costume designer A person who designs the clothing that is worn by characters in a play, film, or television show.

darkroom technician A person who makes sure that chemicals, paper, and other necessary materials are in the darkroom, where negatives are developed.

fashion designer A person who designs clothing.

fashion line A group of clothes that a designer or store offers for a season.

fashion photographer A person who takes fashion pictures.

fashion show coordinator A person who displays a fashion line at a show or event. This person is responsible for making sure all elements of the show run smoothly.

fashion stylist A person who makes sure that clothing fits the models properly. The stylist makes any necessary adjustments.

figure typing Looking at an individual and determining his or her body type (or shape).

formal modeling The runway show of a fashion line.

hair stylist A person who styles models' hair.

informal modeling Two or three models casually displaying a fashion line, either at a store or at a special event.

image consultant A person who uses fashion to improve a person's self-esteem. Image consultants determine which colors and styles are most flattering to a client.

internship A position that allows a person to learn about a business. Internships usually pay very little, and sometimes nothing at all.

line list A list that details information such as style numbers, price, fabric, and colors of items in a fashion line.

makeup stylist A person who does models' makeup.

merchandising assistant A person who helps put a fashion line together for each season. He or she works from original concept to finished product.

model A person who is employed to display a product by wearing it.

muslin A strong, sheer cotton fabric that's used for sample and production work.

on location A place where a photograph is shot away from the studio.

paper pattern The first pattern made of a new design. Made of paper, it includes the various parts of a garment.

pattern grader A person who takes paper patterns and copies them in different sizes.

personal shopper A person who buys clothes for clients.

photography assistant A person who helps a photographer.

portfolio A collection of a photographer's or designer's best work.

production assistant A person who makes sure that the production and shipping of fashion items go smoothly.

promotions assistant A person who makes sure the public and media are aware of fashion products.

proof sheet A sheet with many small photographs from which a client chooses the photographs he or she wants to use.

retail marketing assistant A person who promotes clothing for a company, often coordinating models and clothing for fashion events.

rough sketches The initial drawings done by a designer. They show details of a new design.

salpe A rubberized material used for accessory samples and production work.

sample A garment that is created to give a designer an idea of how a design will look.

showroom salesperson A person who sells clothing and accessories to showroom customers.

silhouette The outline of a figure or garment.

spreader A person who lays out fabric for garments.

style analysis The examination of a person's coloring, figure, features, and personality to come up with a clothing suitable for him or her.

talent The model or models used for a photo shoot.

visual merchandiser The person who creates displays in retail stores.

white seamless A white, smooth, seamless background used in a photograph.

INDEX